WREKIN ALES PUBS IN AND AROUND SHROPSHIRE

First For Your Thirst!

ALLAN FROST

The History Press

Aerial view of The Wrekin Brewery premises in Market Street, Wellington, Shropshire, as they appeared in the 1950s.

*For those whose glass is always half full
and can remember when pubs were the hub
of town and village life.*

First published 2008
The History Press
The Mill, Brimscombe Port,
Stroud, Gloucestershire, GL5 2QG
www.thehistorypress.co.uk

Reprinted 2009

British Library Cataloguing in Publication Data.
A catalogue record for this book is available from the British Library.

ISBN 978 0 7524 4767 4

Typesetting and origination by The History Press
Printed in Great Britain.

CONTENTS

ACKNOWLEDGEMENTS

Author's collection, A. Athersmith, J. Brown, K. Butcher, R. Collier, P. Garbett, A. Hobbs, S. Lane, S. Lewis, N. Medlicott, D. Murphy, N. Murphy, S. Nabb, T. Neal, C. Rutter, Shropshire Records & Research Centre, *Shropshire Star* (and its helpful readers), R. Sims, *Telford Journal*, C. Webster, *Wellington Journal & Shrewsbury News*, Wellington Library, W. Wolfendale. The photograph of the Black Lion Inn at Llanfair Caereinion is reproduced with permission from *The Photographer in Rural Wales* by W. T. R. Pryce (Powysland Club 1991); those of the Fleece and Plough at Knighton appear in *Pubs of Radnorshire* and that of the New Inn, Ludlow from *Pubs of Ludlow and Neighbouring Villages*, both by Tony Hobbs and published by Logaston Press. I am most grateful to them all, as well as for the unfailing support of my wife Dorothy, and apologise sincerely to anyone who has been inadvertently omitted. Every effort has been made to correctly identify the facts, dates, events and people portrayed in the illustrations.

Aerial view of Murphy's Pop Works (formerly The Shropshire Brewery), 1950s. It was here that beers, ales, mineral waters and even milk were bottled for distribution to Wrekin Ales public houses.

INTRODUCTION

The Wrekin Brewery of Wellington in Shropshire has a long, fascinating history. Founded in 1870, it was taken over in 1966 by Greenall Whitley of Warrington. Beer production continued until 1969 when the brewery was closed. The buildings were demolished in 1975 to make way for retail developments.

Like many late Victorian breweries, The Wrekin Brewery struggled to survive against competition from other breweries in the town as well as elsewhere. It seemed destined for closure until it was acquired in 1921 by a man with vision and a strong business head on his shoulders: Owen Downey Murphy, who preferred to be known simply as 'O.D.'.

With O.D.'s hand at the helm, The Wrekin Brewery embarked on a journey of public house acquisition which continued throughout its remaining history. O.D. was succeeded by his sons Ronald and Graham, and even his grandson Duncan became a director of the company in 1962.

What is largely forgotten nowadays is that The Wrekin Brewery became the largest privately owned brewery in the country, a fact which made it an extremely attractive prospect for a number of national breweries seeking not only to quash competition but also expand their spheres of operation, both regionally as well as by adding more public houses to their portfolios.

By the 1950s, The Wrekin Brewery owned more than 200 public houses, mainly in Shropshire but also extending into neighbouring counties and mid-Wales. It was an astonishing accomplishment. To achieve such a position wasn't easy, yet because O.D. had earlier acquired The Shropshire Brewery (also in Wellington), thus enabling him to use its bottling facilities for the production of soft drinks, and an important spirit licence by which he was able to supply his own pubs with the full range of beverages, he managed to place the brewery in an economically strong position. Ultimately, the success of the Murphy family in building up such an enviable empire led to its downfall.

This book is collection of photographs of those public houses and hotels which, at one time or another, came under Wrekin Brewery ownership. It is not intended to be a history of those pubs, which would be an enormous task, but rather a visual appreciation of the brewery's outstanding achievement.

Sadly, many of the buildings included here have changed their use or been demolished over the last fifty years and, whereas it has not been possible to obtain photographs of each and every public house in The Wrekin Brewery portfolio (a few, like The Nelson on Bridgnorth Road at Madeley, which last renewed its licence in 1901, disappeared over 100 years ago before photography became commonplace), I have managed to find approximately 215 from a total of 231.

I hope you find them interesting.

Above left: The original premises of The Wrekin Brewery as they appeared in 1900 and, *right,* in 2007. The building is now used as an amusement arcade.

The second and final brewery building with its workforce, casks and drays, early 1900s.

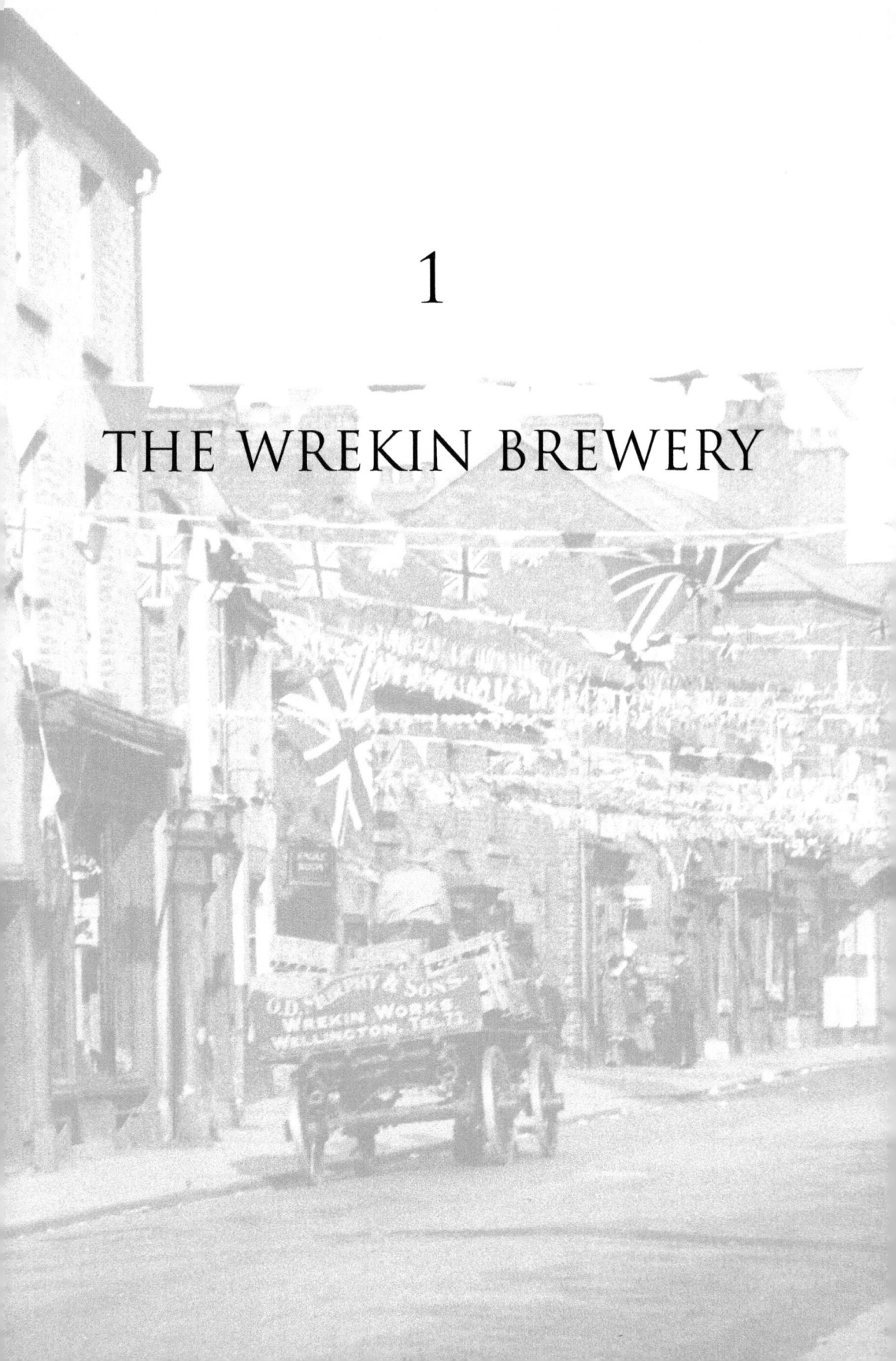

1

THE WREKIN BREWERY

The Wrekin Brewery first began beer and ale production in Market Street, Wellington, in 1870. Some ten years later it moved to new, larger premises a little further down the road and remained there until its closure.

O.D. Murphy began manufacturing mineral waters at Long's Brewery in Ironbridge in 1904. At this early stage in his career he concentrated on bottling soft drinks as this is what he understood best from earlier experience gained as a salesman for R. White & Son of Smethwick. Unfortunately, Ironbridge was not the best location for business expansion, situated as it is in a valley, a fact which rendered it impossible to haul wagon loads of full bottles up hills to potential customers. Consequently, he moved to Wellington in 1907 and took over an existing mineral-water works on Mill Bank. Soon afterwards, he occupied The Botanical Brewery in Watling Street, again not to brew beer but to make use of its bottling facilities.

Wishing to expand the business further, he acquired the former Shropshire Brewery on Holyhead Road from Butler & Co. of Wolverhampton, who had themselves purchased the brewery a year earlier solely to increase its tied public house portfolio. Furthermore, to minimise the risk of competition, they imposed a restriction that brewing should not take place on the premises in future.

As it happened, O.D. was only interested in acquiring The Shropshire Brewery for its bottling facilities and the space it gave for future growth. As time went by, he not only bottled his own soft drinks and milk from the cattle on his farms but also gained contracts from major beer, ale and mineral-water producers to bottle their own drinks. These included Guinness, Bass, Ind Coope and Worthington.

Seeing there was money to be made in producing alcoholic drinks, O.D. decided to try his hand at brewing. The opportunity came in 1921 when The Wrekin Brewery came up for sale together with its thirty-three tied houses and sundry other property. Almost immediately, the brewery began to acquire other pubs at a time when ownership of pubs was seen as asking for trouble. Following severe restrictions on brewing and beer distribution during the First World War, many breweries were going to the wall and pub tenants were finding it difficult to make a decent living. It was definitely a buyer's market. O.D. was able to buy licensed properties at unrealistically cheap prices because no one else wanted to take them on. O.D.'s purchase of The Red Lion Brewery, also in Wellington, in 1924 brought another eight pubs under his control and, in order to enhance the importance of The Wrekin Brewery, production of ales at The Red Lion Brewery ceased. Further pubs were added to the brewery's portfolio by the purchase of Creswell's Brewery in Hadley, Shropshire, in 1948.

He also realised that he needed a licence to deal in wines and spirits rather than have to pay someone else to supply his growing number of pubs. In 1929, O.D. bought three Slaney's Vaults outlets at Wellington, Oakengates and Broseley, which came with that much needed licence.

Thus O.D. found himself in the enviable position of being able to produce his own ales and mineral waters, deal in wines and spirits and supply everything a pub needed to provide drinks for its patrons. His hold over the local soft drinks market was further strengthened by the acquisition of other pop manufacturing businesses at Oswestry and Wolverhampton. While it is common practice for modern non-brewing pub chains to dictate whose drinks are sold on their premises, O.D. was well ahead of his time when it came to provisioning beverages for his pubs.

The next major development came with the wider use of motorised transport. Heavily laden horse-drawn drays were not the most efficient method of transporting casks and bottles over long distances, but the purchase of a fleet of pick-up trucks in 1929 meant drinks could be transported quickly and without difficulty.

This led to the purchase of more tied houses, not just in towns along main roads (like Welshpool and Ludlow) but also in out-of-the-way places where the pub was the centre of sleepy village social life. To ensure continued expansion, O.D. (and, after his death in 1943, his sons) kept a watchful eye on auctions taking place in all parts of the country. They knew from experience that pubs in and around Shropshire could be owned by breweries and individuals from as far away as Birmingham and London.

O.D. and his sons understood the importance of advertising and the slogan 'First For Your Thirst' soon became a common sight on brewery pub signs, as did the collective name for their brews: 'Wrekin Ales'. Very few signs included illustrations (although there is evidence to suggest that steps were being taken in the early 1960s to provide pictorial signs for at least a few of their pubs); the Murphys preferred hand-painted green words on a gold background, colours which became the company's corporate identity. The fact that the brewery won several awards for its ales during its latter years strengthened the brand name, as did the production of advertising barware in the form of beer mats, ash trays, water jugs, soda syphons, and, of course, drinking glasses in all shapes and sizes.

It came as no surprise that The Wrekin Brewery found itself the largest privately owned brewery in the country. Several national breweries made overtures to arrange a takeover, especially when rumours of O.D.'s poor health began to circulate. Although these bids were rejected, the situation after the Second World War began to threaten the brewery's long-term prospects for maintaining its independence.

Whereas post-war social activities led to an increase in some aspects of trade, especially in country pubs which could be accessed by more folk motoring around for pleasure, there was a definite trend towards drinking at home. Wines and spirits were becoming increasingly popular, as was a new continental style drink: lager.

Lager requires a different brewing technique to beer and The Wrekin Brewery was not in a position to spend vast sums on new plant and machinery. An attempt at brewing a lager-style beer called *Wrekin Ritter* failed to appeal to a discerning public. Then, just when the Murphys thought things couldn't get any worse, they were presented with plans showing how proposed Dawley (later Telford) New Town development would entail the demolition of some seventy Wrekin pubs within the designated area, without adequate or realistic compensation. The plans also included the building of a mere nine new pubs, ownership of which would be put to tender. There is no doubt the New Town Development Corporation, with its far-reaching powers of land and property acquisition, saw its role as one of creating an artificial middling class conurbation, one in which there was no room for working class pubs. It would not take long for carpets to replace tiles on the floors in many, but fortunately not all, public house bars.

As The Wrekin Brewery could only hope to acquire one or two (the rest being snapped up by wealthy national concerns), it added insult to injury. There was little choice but to negotiate with Ansells, Allied, Ind Coope, Tetley Walker and Greenall Whitley and accept the consequences.

Greenall Whitley won the bidding but was, it appears, only interested in acquiring the 200 or so Wrekin Ales houses, and had no desire to continue brewing beers or manufacturing soft drinks in Wellington. Beer production ultimately transferred to Wem Brewery, whereupon 'Wem Ales' and 'Greenall Whitley' replaced 'Wrekin Ales' and 'Wrekin Brewery' on pub signs. It would not take long for uneconomic, out-of-the-way pubs to be closed down for good, whatever the social consequences – The Fleece Inn at Knighton was one of the first to go.

So, after 100 years in brewing, The Wrekin Brewery shut its doors for the last time in 1969.

For a fully illustrated history of The Wrekin Brewery, see *Breweries and Bottlers of Wellington* by this author (The History Press, 2008).

Lot.	Situation.			Description.				Tenant.
1 A.	Wellington	..		Red Lion Brewery	..	..	..	In hand.
	Do.	..	..	Offices and Cottage	..	..	..	Ditto and Mr. Adlington.
B.	Do.	..	..	Maltings and Land	..	..	..	In Hand.
	Do.	..	..	Garage	..	..	..	Mr. O. D. Murphy.
C.	Do.	..	..	Red Lion Inn and Outbuildings	..		..	Manager.
D.	Do.	..	..	" The Red Lion " and Outbuildings		..	..	Mr. J. Round.
	Do.	..	..	Cottage	..	..	..	Mr. Cotton,
E.	Dawley	..	..	" The Talbot," and Outbuildings	..		..	Mr. R. Picken.
	Do.	..		Dwelling House and Shop		..	..	Mr. P. G. Perkins.
	Do.	..	..	Cottage	..	..	..	Mr. R. Picken.
F.	St. Georges	..	..	Swan Inn and Outbuildings		..	..	Mr. T. E. Hordley.
G.	Oakengates	..	..	" The Charlton " and Outbuildings			..	Manager.
	Do.	..	..	The Charlton Ground	..		..	Oakengates F.C.
	Do.	..	..	Dwelling House and Shop		..	..	Mr. J. Bagnall.
	Do.	..	..	Detached Shop	..		..	Mr. W. Lloyd.
	Do.	..	..	Outbuildings	..	..	..	Various users.
H.	New Hadley	..	..	" The Granville Arms "	..		..	Mr. J. Sutton or Successor.
I.	Trench	..	..	Crown Inn	..	..	..	Manager or Successor.
J.	Shrewsbury	..		" The Wheatsheaf "	..	..	..	Mrs. Buttery.
	Do.	..	..	Cottages	..	..	..	North and others.
2	Battlefield	..	..	" The Red Lion " &c.	..	..	..	Mr. A. G. Rowlinson.
3	New Hadley	..	..	Eight Cottages	..	..	..	Messrs. Price and others.
4	Do.	..	..	Garden Ground	..	..	..	Mr. J. Sutton or Successor.
5	Wellington	..	..	Eight Cottages and Land		..	..	Messrs Evans, Harper, Roberts, Walker, Corbett, Robinson, Williams & Jones.
6	Do.	..	..	Eight Ditto.	..	..	..	Messrs. Davies, Gough, Powis, Davies, Stokes, Podd and Westwick.

Summary of Particulars for O.D.'s acquisition of The Red Lion Brewery, 1924, showing the public houses and other properties included in the sale.

One of the fleet of pick-up trucks operating from the Pop Works in Holyhead Road, Wellington, 1929.

Above left: An O.D. Murphy horse-drawn dray in High Street, Wellington, 1935. *Above right:* Renovations are undertaken at The Rock House, Farley (near Much Wenlock) during 1936.

A Wrekin Brewery dray delivers casks at The Haygate, Wellington, *c.* 1960.

Signs of the times. *Above left:* The Last Inn at Church Aston with lettering which says, 'All this long day I have sought for good ale & at The Last I have found it.' *Above right:* A new sign sample created during 1962.

Ronald Murphy in his vintage 1905 Panhard Levassor car visits All Labour in Vain, Horsehay, *c.* 1952.

The Royal Oak at Ellerdine is the venue for a shooting party, 1930s. Ron Murphy is third from the left.

Barman Trevor, holding a Wrekin Ales tray, stands in the newly refurbished Open Road bar at the Charlton Arms Hotel, Wellington, 1960s. Mrs Baldwin was manageress at the time.

Opening night at the Old Three Pigeons Inn at Nesscliffe, *c.* 1962. From left to right: Newly appointed director Duncan Murphy, Ron Murphy, Mr McGee (head brewer), the landlord and landlady, Barbara Murphy.

A selection of Wrekin Brewery memorabilia including a mirrored wall clock, old blue-backed playing card, bottle opener, pale-green bar water jug, red serving tray and beermat.

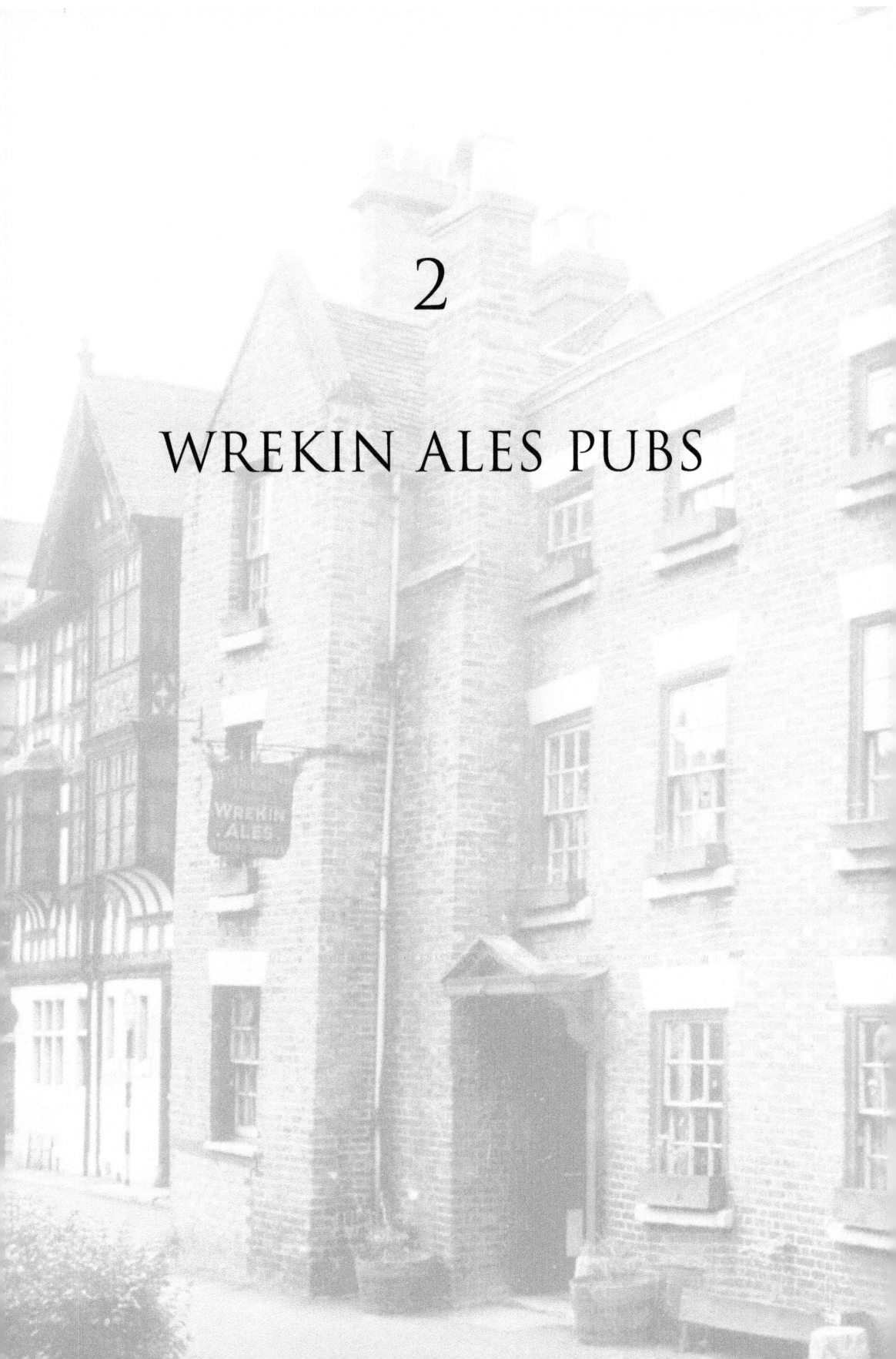

2

WREKIN ALES PUBS

The characteristics of those pubs owned by The Wrekin Brewery varied enormously simply because they were to be found in both large and small towns as well as villages and remote places. Considering the number of public houses in existence in towns throughout the country during the first half of the twentieth century, it is astounding that their tenants managed to make any sort of living.

Having so many public houses and hotels to maintain must have presented many problems to Wrekin Brewery management. Building repairs and general maintenance were an ongoing feature, supplemented by new installations for heating, lighting (electricity was introduced from the 1930s onwards) and pumps to bring ales from the cellar into the bar. In fact, until pumps were installed, ale was carried in jugs filled from casks fitted with taps. In addition to the brewery's own maintenance personnel, specialist plumbing installations were undertaken by outside professionals; for example, plumbing engineer G.H. York of New Street, Wellington. Pointons of Bell Street, also in Wellington, made and painted the signs to hang outside pubs.

Not all pubs were worth the investment or lost their licences to sell alcohol for other reasons; in those circumstances, there was little point in keeping them in the portfolio, so they were sold or demolished to make way for new buildings, although the Murphys rarely built new pubs, much preferring to improve existing ones. Furthermore, a considerable number of pubs were obliged to close because of adverse trading conditions during the First World War and again around 1930. One of the first Wrekin pubs to close, even before the Murphys acquired the brewery, was The Nelson at Madeley, Shropshire, which last applied for a licence in 1901.

Pubs and hotels catered for all tastes. A large number of Wrekin houses were undoubtedly frequented by working-class patrons, many of whom worked in factories and mines. Village and other road-side hostelries relied on local farm workers and passing travellers for their trade. Ever since the late nineteenth century, members of the Cyclists Touring Club (CTC), Automobile Association (AA) and Royal Automobile Club (RAC) kept their eyes open for badges displayed outside public houses, indicating that the premises had been vetted and found sufficiently amenable for club members seeking overnight accommodation. Similarly, several houses advertised themselves as 'Commercial' (frequented by travelling salesmen) and 'Family' (suitable for families). Furthermore, to add appeal to those who did not wish to combine alcohol with driving, teas and coffee were advertised in addition to strong drink.

One particular pub deserves a special mention: the Clive Arms at White Grit, Shropshire. In fact, it was a very small remote farm run by an elderly lady for many years, certainly until the mid 1960s. She used to have one barrel of beer delivered for consumption by a few scattered locals and travellers. The public bar room was so small it became known as 'The Hole and Poker', later abbreviated to 'The Poker'. Eight drinkers filled the room to bursting point.

As time went by, pubs and hotels adapted their facilities to take client preferences and needs into account. From the 1930s onwards, for example, defunct stables were converted into garages or rooms capable of more formal use, like small dining rooms and public toilets. By the 1950s, more and more pubs provided car parks (a few even had petrol pumps!) and offered hot snacks to customers as a welcome addition to the usual packets of crisps, nuts and pork scratchings. Sadly, one-armed bandits and jukeboxes also found their way into bars, thus starting a trend away from the acceptable hubbub of pub chat towards noisy and intrusive cacophony.

Traditionally, pubs were places where games like darts, dominoes, bar billiards, tabletop skittles, shove ha'penny, cards and even crown green bowling were played on a regular basis long before 'quiz nites' and karaoke were introduced. Local leagues enabled teams from pubs in an area to compete against each other, and went some way towards increasing sales on otherwise quiet week nights. But pubs weren't only frequented by the working classes. Members (usually men) from middle- and upper-class backgrounds used them as bases for pursuits like shooting and fishing. Coach parties and ramblers (as long as they removed their boots) were also welcome. The Murphys, of course, often visited their pubs to ensure they were well run; a pub with a bad name could lose its licence as well as its reputation.

Greenall Whitley closed and sold a number of former Wrekin pubs from 1969 onwards, mainly for economic reasons; whereas the Murphys understood the social importance of small pubs to local patrons, it appears Greenall Whitley was more concerned with the financial implications of operating less profitable houses. It is largely because of their attitude and subsequent changes in drinking habits that a considerable number of tied houses no longer exist or, if they are still standing, have changed their appearance almost beyond recognition, especially where they are now owned by national chains like Pubmaster, Punch Taverns and Enterprise Pubs.

Some pubs, like the Tayleur Arms at Longdon on Tern, Shropshire, sold Wrekin Ales but, because they were Free Houses, did not form part of the Wrekin Brewery portfolio. This book contains photographs of premises identified as being owned by The Wrekin Brewery at some point during the century of its existence. They are in alphabetic order by town or village and, where possible, reveal what they looked like at the time they were owned by the brewery. Most are commissioned photographs taken by *The Wellington Journal & Shrewsbury News* during the 1950s to produce brewery calendars. Other photographs have been included where it has not been possible to locate an authentic 'Wrekin Ales' version.

Regrettably, photographs of a comparatively few pubs have eluded the author, sometimes because they ceased to be public houses many years ago or have been demolished. There is, of course, always the possibility of further photographs coming to light: records of Wrekin public houses are virtually non-existent and not every hostelry was retained for a long period, so there may be a few more yet to be discovered. Nevertheless, those included in the following pages give more than a fair representation of the types of properties providing 'First For Your Thirst' refreshment to patrons over many years.

A sign of change: the landlord's name is obliterated from the statutory notice above a pub doorway, either when a new landlord is about to be appointed or the pub has lost its licence.

BERRINGTON, Herefordshire, Bell Inn	ORETON Plough Inn
BROSELEY Hand and Tankard	PRESTHORPE Plough Inn
BROSELEY (High Street) Vaults Inn	ST GEORGES (Gower Street) Bell Inn
CLEE HILL Dhu Stone Inn	ST GEORGES (West Street) Gate Inn
LEEGOMERY Red House (Off Licence)	TRENCH Crown Inn
LINLEY BROOK Fox and Hounds	WELSHPOOL (High Street) The Mermaid
MADELEY (Bridgnorth Road) The Nelson	WELSHPOOL 'Upper' Pheasant
NEW INVENTION (Bucknell), Stag's Head	WELSHPOOL (Berriew Street) Wellington Inn

List of the few Wrekin Ales public houses for which no photographs have been obtained.

Abermule, Powys: The Waterloo Arms Hotel, early 1950s.

Admaston, Shropshire: The Pheasant, mid-1950s.

Allscott, Shropshire: The Plough Inn, early 1960s.

Bagginswood, Shropshire: The Crown Inn, mid-1950s.

Battlefield, Shrewsbury, Shropshire: The Red Lion Inn, mid-1950s.

Berriew (Brithdir), Powys: The Horseshoe Inn, late 1950s.

Bettws, Powys: The New Inn, late 1950s.

Beverley, Shropshire: The Compasses Inn, early 1960s.

Bishops Castle (Welsh Street), Shropshire: The Black Lion Inn, mid-1950s.

Bishops Castle (Church Street), Shropshire: The Six Bells Inn, mid-1950s.

Bratton, Shropshire: The Gate, *c.* 1964.

Bridgnorth (Northgate), Shropshire: The Bear Inn, *c.* 1964.

Bridgnorth (Cartway), Shropshire: The Black Boy during Coronation celebrations, 1953.

Bridgnorth (Whitburn Street), Shropshire: The Carpenters Arms, *c.* 1963.

Bridgnorth (Alverley), Shropshire: The Squirrel Inn, mid-1950s.

Bridgnorth (Mill Street), Shropshire: The Vine Inn, late 1950s.

Broome, Shropshire: The Engine & Tender, early 1960s.

Broseley (High Street), Shropshire: The Albion Inn, mid-1950s.

Broseley (King Street), Shropshire: The Cumberland Hotel, as seen in 1959. The hotel was opened in 1948 having been a private residence since it was built in 1714. It was bought by The Wrekin Brewery for £3,000.

Broseley, (King Street) Shropshire: Duke of Cumberland Inn, 1940s. The inn's licence was transferred in 1948 to The Cumberland Hotel *(top)* whereupon The Duke ceased to be a public house.

Broseley, Shropshire: The Duke of York, 1965.

Broseley, (King Street), Shropshire: The King's Head Inn, 1960.

Broseley, (Benthall), Shropshire: The New Inn after a fire in the 1990s when it was a free house.

Caersws, Powys: The Unicorn Hotel in 1961.

Canon Pyon, Herefordshire: The Nag's Head in 1963.

Church Aston (Newport), Shropshire: The Last Inn, 1959.

Church Eaton, Shropshire: The Royal Oak, 1964.

Church Stretton (High Street), Shropshire: The King's Arms as seen in 1955.

Clee Hill, Shropshire: The Golden Cross, 1958.

Clee Hill, Shropshire: The Victoria Inn, 1958.

Clun, Shropshire: The White Horse Inn, 1962.

Clunton, Shropshire: The Crown Inn, 1956.

Coalbrookdale (Wellington Road), Shropshire: The Coalbrookdale Inn, 1960.

Coalbrookdale, Shropshire: The Valley Hotel. Originally built by master collier George Goodwin as a residence in 1757. This photograph was taken in 1958.

Coalport, Shropshire: The Brewery Inn, 1960.

Coalport (High Street), Shropshire: The
Shakespeare Inn, *c.* 1955.

Coalport, Shropshire: The Woodbridge Hotel, 1962.

Cold Hatton, Shropshire: The Seven Stars in 1956.

Crackley Bank, Shropshire: The Hare & Hounds, as it was in 1957.

TEAS

THE EAGLES
WREKIN ALES
WINES & SPIRITS
Refreshments

Cressage, Shropshire: The Eagles, 1955.

Cross Houses, Shropshire: The Bell Hotel, 1959.

Culmington, Shropshire: The Royal Oak, now a private house, as seen in 1957.

Dawley (Bank), Shropshire: The Old Red Lion as it was in 1961.

Dawley (Bank Road), Shropshire: The Queen's Arms, 1965.

Above: Dawley (Burton Street), Shropshire: The Royal Exchange in 1962.

Left: The Wrekin Hotel, the brewery's flagship hostelry was erected in Market Square, Wellington, in the late 1960s. It occupied ground formerly used, among other things, as a candle factory which burned down in 1865 causing severe damage to neighbouring properties. The hotel, seen here during the 1890s, appears to have closed sometime after 1916, when it is last mentioned in trade directories.

Dawley (High Street), Shropshire: The Talbot Inn as it appeared in the mid-1950s.

Dawley (Finger Road), Shropshire: The White Horse as it appears today.

Dawley (Heath Hill), Shropshire: The White Horse, *c.* 1956.

Dawley (Little), Shropshire: The Red Lion.

Dawley (Little), Shropshire: The Unicorn Inn, as seen in October 2007.

Donnington Wood, Shropshire: The Bell Inn, 1959.

Dorrington (Walford Bridge), Shropshire: The Bridge Inn in the mid-1950s.

Dorrington, Shropshire: The Horse Shoes, 1956.

Eardisland, Herefordshire: The White Swan in 1964.

Eccleshall, Staffordshire: The Freemason's Arms, 1956.

Eccleshall, Staffordshire: The Railway Inn, 1961.

Edgmond, Shropshire: The Lamb, 1957.

Ellerdine Heath, Shropshire: The Royal Oak. See also the photograph on page 15.

Farley, near Much Wenlock, Shropshire: The Rock Inn in 1934, shortly after it had been acquired by The Wrekin Brewery. Considerable renovations were necessary (see photograph on page 13) as well as a new extension to bring the property up to scratch (see next photograph).

Farley, near Much Wenlock, Shropshire: The Rock Inn as it appeared in the 1950s.

Ford, Shropshire: The Cross Gates, 1955.

Glynceiriog, North Wales: The Glyn Valley Hotel, 1964.

Great Chatwell, Shropshire: The Red Lion Inn, 1960.

Hadley (Trench Lock), Shropshire: The Barley Mow, 1959.

Hadley (Trench Lock), Shropshire: The Bull's Head, 1961.

Hadley (High Street), Shropshire: The Cross Keys Inn, 1962.

Hadley, New (Hadley Road), Shropshire: The Granville Arms, 1965, formerly a Red Lion Brewery house acquired by The Wrekin Brewery in 1924.

Hanwood, Shropshire: The Cock Inn, 1963.

Harlech, Gwynedd: The Queen's Hotel, as seen in 2007. The Wrekin Brewery added a toilet block in 1952 and re-roofed it in 1963. The hotel was the furthest away from the brewery's base in Wellington and is now run by Nikki Medlicott and Stuart Lane.

Harmer Hill, Shropshire: Red Castle Inn, 1964.

Hinkshay, Shropshire: The White Hart, *c.* 1950. The pub finally closed in 2006 and suffered tremendous fire damage in March 2007, after which it became derelict and vandalised.

Hinstock, Shropshire: The Falcon Inn, seen as a Free House after Greenall Whitley sold it in the 1970s.

Hook-a-Gate, Shropshire: The Royal Oak, 1957.

Hopton Bank, Hopton Wafers, Shropshire: The Miner's Arms, 1960s, with landlady Edith Astbury. The pub was known locally as 'The Lady's Finger', for reasons unknown. It closed in 1972, having been licensed since 1830. The Astbury family had run it from 1940.

Horderley, Shropshire: The Red Lion, 1956.

Horsehay, Shropshire: All Labour In Vain, 1956 (compare with the photograph on page 14). Several structural alterations were made to the building during the intervening period.

Horton, Shropshire: Queen's Head, 1962.

Ironbridge (Madeley Road), Shropshire: George & Dragon, mid-1950s.

Ironbridge (Jockey Bank), Shropshire: Horse and Jockey, mid-1950s.

Ironbridge (High Street), Shropshire: Queen's Head (on the left), probably during the 1950s.

Ironbridge (Waterloo Street), Shropshire: Robin Hood Inn, 1961.

Ironbridge, Shropshire: Station Hotel, 1965.

Ironbridge (The Wharfage), Shropshire: Swan Hotel, 1957, which became an inn in 1759 and was granted a full licence in 1791.

Ironbridge (The Wharfage), Shropshire: Talbot Inn, 1965. Its licence dates from before 1844.

Ironbridge (The Wharfage), Shropshire: White Hart Hotel, 1959. It was a coaching inn in 1851.

Ironbridge (Lincoln Hill), Shropshire: White Horse, 1962. The first known licensee was Benjamin Bennett in the 1820s.

Jackfield, Shropshire: Tumbling Sailor (or 'Sailors'). Built on a bank of the River Severn, the premises were prone to flooding, as this 2004 photograph shows. It is now a private house.

Kemberton, Shropshire: Masons Arms, mid-1950s.

Kerry, Powys: The Herbert Arms.

THE HORSESHOE INN
KETLEY
1½ Miles from Wellington on the A.5
WREKIN'S FINEST ALES

BACKGROUND MUSIC
LIVE WEEKEND MUSIC
SPACIOUS LOUNGE AND HOMELY BAR
FRONT AND REAR CAR PARKS FOR FIFTY CARS

*YOU ARE SURE OF A "JOLLY" GOOD WELCOME
FROM LEN AND RITA JOLLY, PROPRIETORS.*

Early 1960s advertisement for The Horseshoe Inn (sometimes known as The Horse Shoes), Ketley (Holyhead Road), Shropshire.

Ketley (Holyhead Road), Shropshire: The Horse Shoes, 1957.

Ketley (Holyhead Road), Shropshire: the original Seven Stars, built in 1579.

Ketley (Holyhead Road), Shropshire: The new Seven Stars shortly after being built in 1964. It was later demolished and the Elephant & Castle built on the site. Note the advertising slogan on the bus.

Ketley Bank (Main Road), Shropshire: Stafford Arms, 1965.

Kinlet, Shropshire: Eagle & Serpent, 1958.

Kinnerley, Shropshire: Cross Keys, 1963.

Knighton, Powys: The Fleece Inn, 1953, which closed in 1969 and is now a guest house.

Knighton, Powys: The Plough.

Knighton, Powys: Swan Hotel, mid-1950s.

Leighton, Shropshire: Kynnersley Arms, 1957.

Leintwardine, Shropshire: Swan Hotel, 1957.

Lingen, Herefordshire: The Rose and Crown, 1965.

Lingen, Herefordshire: The Royal George, early 1960s.

Linley Brook (near Astley Abbotts), Bridgnorth, Shropshire: The Pheasant Inn, 1964.

Little Stretton, Shropshire: The Green Dragon Hotel, 1956.

Little Wenlock, Shropshire: The Huntsman, 1964.

Little Wenlock, Shropshire: The Spread Eagles, 1955.

Llandrinio, Powys: The Punch Bowl, 1964.

Llandyssil, Powys: Upper House Inn, as seen in the 1930s.

Llanfair Caereinion, Powys: The Black Lion as photographed in the 1880s. The pub is located in the narrow lane to the left of the market hall.

Llanidloes (Great Oak Street), Powys: Angel Hotel as seen in the 1930s. The pub was built in 1714.

Above: Llanidloes, Powys: Another view of Angel Hotel, 1963. Compare the enlarged windows with those in the previous photograph.

Left: Llanymynech, Powys: Dolphin Hotel, 1956.

Long Lane (near Wellington), Shropshire: The Buck's Head, 1955.

Ludlow (Lower Broad Street), Shropshire: The Barley Mow, mid-1950s.

Ludlow (Market Street), Shropshire: Globe Inn, 1965.

Ludlow (Upper Galdeford), Shropshire: The New Inn around 1910, now a 'fish bar and restaurant'.

Ludlow (Upper Galdeford), Shropshire: Portcullis Inn, 1960.

Ludlow (Church Street), Shropshire: Rose & Crown Inn, 1958.

Ludlow (Corve Street), Shropshire: The Unicorn, 2002.

Madeley, Shropshire: Beacon Hotel, mid-1950s.

Madeley (High Street), Shropshire: Foresters Arms, early 1960s.

Madeley, Shropshire: The Heart of Oak Inn with its white sign lies centre left; it was demolished in the late 1960s, having been licensed from 1844.

Madeley (Park Lane), Shropshire: The New Inn, shortly before demolition in 1969.

Madeley (Prince Street), Shropshire: Prince of Wales, early 1960s.

Madeley (Station Road), Shropshire: Railway Inn.

Madeley (Church Street), Shropshire: Six Bells, as it appeared in 1977.

Madeley (Church Street), Shropshire: Front view of the Six Bells, as seen in 2007.

Madeley (Bridgnorth Road), Shropshire: Three Furnaces, early 1900s.

Madeley (Bridgnorth Road), Shropshire: Three Furnaces, owned by Enterprise Inns in 2007 when it was advertising for a new manager..

Maesbury, Shropshire: The Original Ball, 1963.

Manafon, Powys: The Beehive Inn in the 1930s after its acquisition by The Wrekin Brewery.

Manafon, Powys: The Beehive Inn, 1959.

Minsterley, Shropshire: Bath Arms Hotel, 1960.

Montgomery, Powys: The Crown Hotel, 1961.

Much Wenlock, Shropshire: Talbot Inn, 1958.

Nesscliffe, Shropshire: The Old Three Pigeons, 1961 (see page 16 for an interior photograph).

Newport (High Street), Shropshire: Barley Mow Hotel, 1958.

Newport (High Street), Shropshire: The Plume of Feathers, 1960.

New Radnor, Radnorshire: Eagle Hotel, 1964.

Newtown, Powys: Angel Vaults, 1959.

Newtown, Powys: Cambrian Vaults, probably in the 1930s after acquisition by The Wrekin Brewery.

Newtown, Powys: Lion Hotel, 1961.

Nordley, Shropshire: Swan Inn, 1963.

Oakengates (Lion Street), Shropshire: Brown Lion Inn, 1960.

Oakengates (Church Street), Shropshire: Charlton Arms, a former Red Lion Brewery house acquired by The Wrekin Brewery in 1924.

Oakengates (Market Street), Shropshire: Crown Inn, 1958.

Oakengates (Market Street), Shropshire: Green Inn, 1950s.

Oakengates (Holyhead Road), Shropshire: Omnibus Inn, 1958. It is now called The Hare & Hounds.

Oakengates (Holyhead Road), Shropshire: Pear Tree Bridge Inn, 1957.

Oakengates (Market Street), Shropshire: Slaney's Vaults, one of three Slaney's Wine and Spirit outlets acquired by The Wrekin Brewery in 1929. It is the white building in the distance.

Oreton, Shropshire: New Inn, early 1960s.

Oswestry, Shropshire: The Willow Tree, mid-1950s.

Oswestry (Llynclys), Shropshire: White Lion Inn, 1958.

Pennal (Machynlledd), Powys: Riverside Hotel, 1961.

Presteigne, Powys: The Barley Mow, mid-1950s.

Presteigne, Powys: The Royal Oak, 1965.

Priorslee (Shifnal Road), Shropshire: The Lion Inn, 1958.

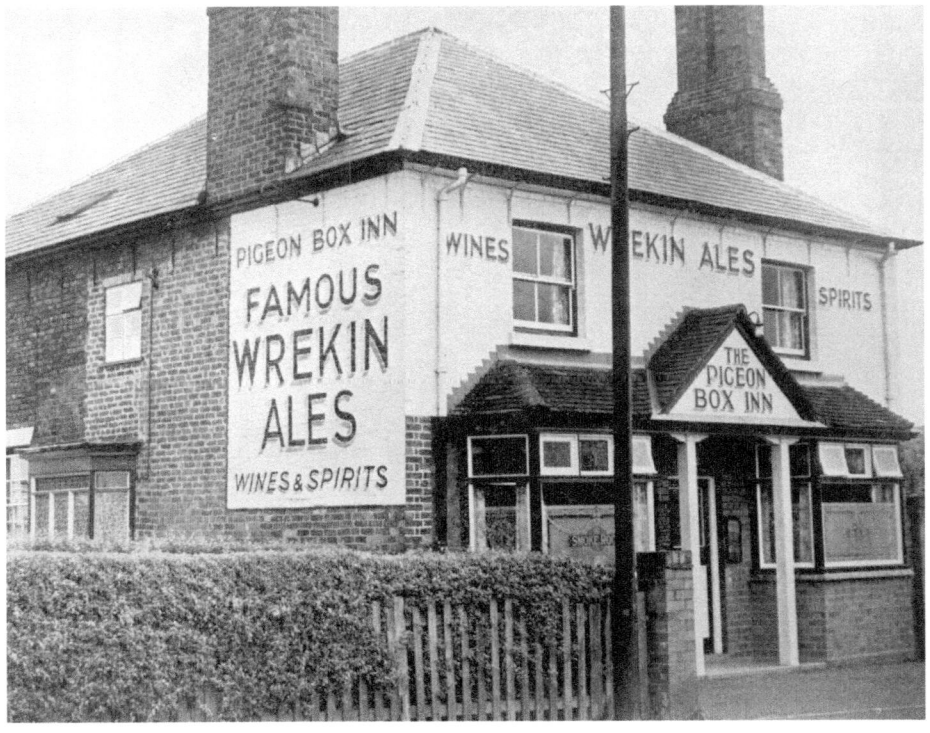

Priorslee (Priorslee Road), Shropshire: The Pigeon Box Inn, 1958.

Richards Castle, Herefordshire: Castle Inn, 1957.

Rodington, Shropshire: Bull's Head, mid-1950s.

Above: Rodington, Shropshire: The Crown Inn, 1971, when Greenall Whitley intended to close the pub. Former 'Wrekin Ales' signs have been replaced by 'Wem Ales' with the Greenall Whitley logo.

Right: Shifnal, Shropshire: Jerningham Arms Hotel, 1955. It has now been converted into apartments.

Shifnal, Shropshire: Star Hotel, 1958.

Shifnal, Shropshire: Union Inn, 1960.

Shrewsbury (Frankwell), Shropshire: The Anchor Inn, January 2008, when the pub was owned by Punch Taverns and managed by Ellen Brannan and Mandy Bishton.

Shrewsbury (Castle Gates), Shropshire: Castle Vaults, 1965, next door to the Hung Hing Chinese restaurant.

Shrewsbury (Frankwell), Shropshire: Wheatsheaf Inn, 1965.

Shrewsbury (The Column/Wenlock Road), The White Horse, 2008, now an Enterprise Inns house.

Shrewsbury (St Mary's Place), Shropshire: Ye Olde Yorkshire House.

St Georges (West Street), Shropshire: The Bush Inn as it appeared in 2007.

St Georges (Church Street), Shropshire: Cottage Spring Inn, 1960.

St Georges (West Street), Shropshire: The George, acquired by Greenall Whitley from the Shrewsbury & Wem Brewery in 1967 to sell Wrekin Ales. The Bush Inn, another Wrekin pub, lies on the opposite side of the road to the left.

Above: St Georges (Church Street), Shropshire: The Quarry House Inn, now called the Ball and Bails, 1950s.

Right: St Georges (West Street), Shropshire: the Swan Inn, now a private dwelling.

Stirchley, Shropshire: The Rose & Crown hosts a fox hunt during the 1950s.

Stottesdon, Shropshire: The Cock Inn, 1950s.

Tenbury Wells, Worcestershire: The Bridge Inn (also known as Hotel), 1960.

Tenbury Wells, Worcestershire: Pembroke House, 1962.

Trench, Shropshire: The Duke of York, 1962.

Uffington, Shropshire: The Corbet Arms, 1956.

Walcot, Shropshire: The Grove Inn, 1955.

Waters Upton, Shropshire: The Swan Inn, 1957.

Wellington (Bell Street), Shropshire: The Barley Mow as it was in May 1960.

Wellington (King Street), Shropshire: The Black Horse, 1960.

Wellington (Haygate Road), Shropshire: The Bull Inn is one of the properties to the right of this late 1920s photograph. It was subsequently demolished to clear the ground for the new Haygate Hotel.

Wellington (Church Street), Shropshire: The Charlton Arms Hotel, 1955. The hotel derives its name from the family who owned Apley Castle on the northern outskirts of the town.

Wellington (New Street), Shropshire: The Duke of Wellington, May 1960. Since demolition, the site has been home to a Gateway supermarket and Bewise economy store.

Wellington (High Street), Shropshire: The Duke's Head, commonly known as 'The Bottles', as it looked in May 1960.

Wellington (Market Street), Shropshire: The Ercall Hotel, 1958. The building is now head office of the Wellington Markets Co.

Wellington (Crown Street), Shropshire: The Fox & Hounds in May 1960.

Wellington (Glebe Street), Shropshire: The Glebe Inn, 1969, shortly before closure.

Wellington (Haygate Road), Shropshire: The Haygate Hotel, one of a few houses actually built by The Wrekin Brewery during the 1930s.

Wellington, Shropshire. *Above left:* (Orleton Lane): Jubilee Stores, a former Wrekin Brewery off licence, as seen in 2007. *Above right:* (New Street): The Lamb, which closed in 1960.

Wellington (High Street), Shropshire: The Nelson Inn, 1960. Demolition followed.

Wellington (Market Street), Shropshire: The Pheasant Inn, 1963.

Wellington (Mill Bank), Shropshire: The Railway Inn, 1963. The premises subsequently expanded to incorporate Stokes butchers' building on the left.

Wellington (High Street), Shropshire: The Red Lion Inn on the extreme right as seen in 1960. The inn closed around 1930. The former Red Lion Brewery in King Street took its name from the pub.

Wellington (Whitchurch Road), Shropshire: The Red Lion Inn, 1961, renamed the Wellington Arms in 2007. Its original name will hopefully be restored.

Wellington (Bell Street), Shropshire: The Rose & Crown, May 1960.

Wellington (Market Square), Shropshire: Slaney's Vaults (otherwise known as the Bradford Arms), mid-1960s.

Wellington, Shropshire: The Smithfield Inn, 1965, once a popular venue for farmers attending weekly Smithfield livestock auctions held over the road until they ceased in 1989.

Welshpool (Broad Street), Powys: The Boar's Head Hotel, 1963.

Wenlock Edge, Shropshire: The Plough Inn, 1957.

Wheathill, Shropshire: The Three Horseshoes Inn, mid-1950s.

Wheaton Aston, Staffordshire: The Hare & Hounds Inn, which closed in 1935 when its licence was transferred to the new Spread Eagles at Gailey. An underground stream kept casks in the cellar cool, and beer was served in jugs. The pub was also a farm where horses were cart trained.

Wigmore, Shropshire: The Compasses Inn, 1963.

Wistanstow, Shropshire: The Plough in 1956. Its present owner, the Wood family, has run its own brewery on the site since 1980.

Withington, Shropshire: The Hare & Hounds, 1961.

Woodseaves, Staffordshire: The Anchor Inn on the Shropshire Union Canal, 2007. The site is now a caravan and camping park and has been run by the same family for over 100 years.

Wrockwardine Wood (Moss Road), Shropshire: The Lamb Inn, 1959.

Wrockwardine Wood, (Lincoln Road) Shropshire: The Pheasant Inn as it appeared in 2007.

Wrockwardine Wood, Shropshire: The Red Lion, 1964.

A variety of pub advertisements from the early to mid-1960s.

Other local titles published by The History Press

Breweries and Bottlers of Wellington
ALLAN FROST

With a full account from medieval times until brewing and bottling ceased in 1969, this book explores the business successes and failures of The Shropshire, The Mill Field, The Red Lion, The Union, The Botanical and The Wrekin Brewery. The origins and subsequent fortunes of small bottling firms are covered as well as the various mineral-water manufacturers who struggled to survive until the Murphy family quashed all competition.

978 0 7524 4631 8

Shropshire Inn Signs
ALAN ROSE

Inn signs have been an enduring part of the British landscape for over 2,000 years and have provided the public with an illustrative depiction of the name of the pub outside which they hang. This book takes the reader on a tour of Shropshire's inns past and present, discovering the origins of names such as The Winning Post, The Trout and The Blue Boar. Illustrated with over 100 images, it offers a fascinating insight into the history of these highly crafted items.

978 0 7524 3843 6

The Wrekin Hill
ALLAN FROST

As well as being the county's most famous landmark offering stunning views from its summit, The Wrekin is a hill steeped in legend. It was, and still is, a playground for people, many of whom still visit its famous Halfway House. This book not only gives a fascinating insight into the unique history of a hill whose name has spread throughout the world but also includes an abundance of illustrations and photographs which will nurture feelings of nostalgia.

978 0 7524 4256 3

Wellington in the 1940s and '50s
ALLAN FROST

This collection of archive photographs documents life in the historic Shropshire market town of Wellington during and after the Second World War. Entertaining and informative, this book reveals how the people of Wellington coped with severe rationing and how they found enjoyment in a wide range of activities. *Wellington in the 1940s and '50s* is an important pictorial history which will delight all who have lived or worked here.

978 0 7524 3767 5

If you are interested in purchasing other books published by The History Press, or in case you have difficulty finding any History Press books in your local bookshop, you can also place orders directly through our website www.thehistorypress.co.uk